MAGNETS PUSH MAGNETS PULL

BY DAVID A. ADLER

ILLUSTRATED BY ANNA RAFF

Holiday House / New York

For Leah,
welcome to our family
—D.A.A.

For Bea and Restawhile
—A.R.

Text copyright © 2017 by David A. Adler
Illustrations copyright © 2017 by Anna Raff
All Rights Reserved
HOLIDAY HOUSE is registered in the U.S. Patent and Trademark Office.
Printed and Bound in November 2016 at Toppan Leefung, DongGuan City, China.
The artwork was created with ink washes, assembled and colored digitally.
www.holidayhouse.com
First Edition
1 3 5 7 9 10 8 6 4 2

Library of Congress Cataloging-in-Publication Data

Names: Adler, David A., author. | Raff, Anna, illustrator.
Title: Magnets push, magnets pull / by David A. Adler; illustrated by Anna Raff.
Description: First edition. | New York: Holiday House, [2017] | Audience:
5-8. | Audience: K to 3.
Identifiers: LCCN 2016027034| ISBN 9780823436699 (hardcover)
ISBN 0823436691 (hardcover)
Subjects: LCSH: Magnets—Juvenile literature. | Magnetism—Juvenile
literature.
Classification: LCC QC757.5.A35 2017 | DDC 538—dc23 LC record available at
https://lccn.loc.gov/2016027034

A world without magnets would be a world without computers, printers, cell phones, televisions, vacuum cleaners and microwave ovens. It's a magnet's invisible pulling and pushing *force* called magnetism that helps power all these devices.

Magnets are attracted to anything made of iron, steel, nickel or cobalt and some less plentiful metals, including neodymium and samarium.

There are two kinds of magnets, *simple magnets* and *electromagnets*. You are probably most familiar with simple magnets, the kind you find in toys or use to hold papers to your refrigerator doors.

Do you have a simple magnet? If you do, you can use it as a metal tester, but be careful with your magnet. Do not bring it close to a watch, clock, computer, television or any delicate instrument. It could damage them.

Test some U.S. coins. Does your magnet stick to any of them? It shouldn't. U.S. coins aren't made mostly of iron, steel, nickel or cobalt. Pennies, nickels, dimes and quarters are mostly copper.

Place your magnet on the hood of a car. Does it stick? It should. Most cars are made from steel.

Take a few cans from your pantry. Does your magnet stick to them? It may stick to some and not to others. Some cans are made of steel. Others are made of aluminum.

Simple magnets come in many shapes and sizes. If you have a magnet of any size, you can use it to test the force of magnetism.

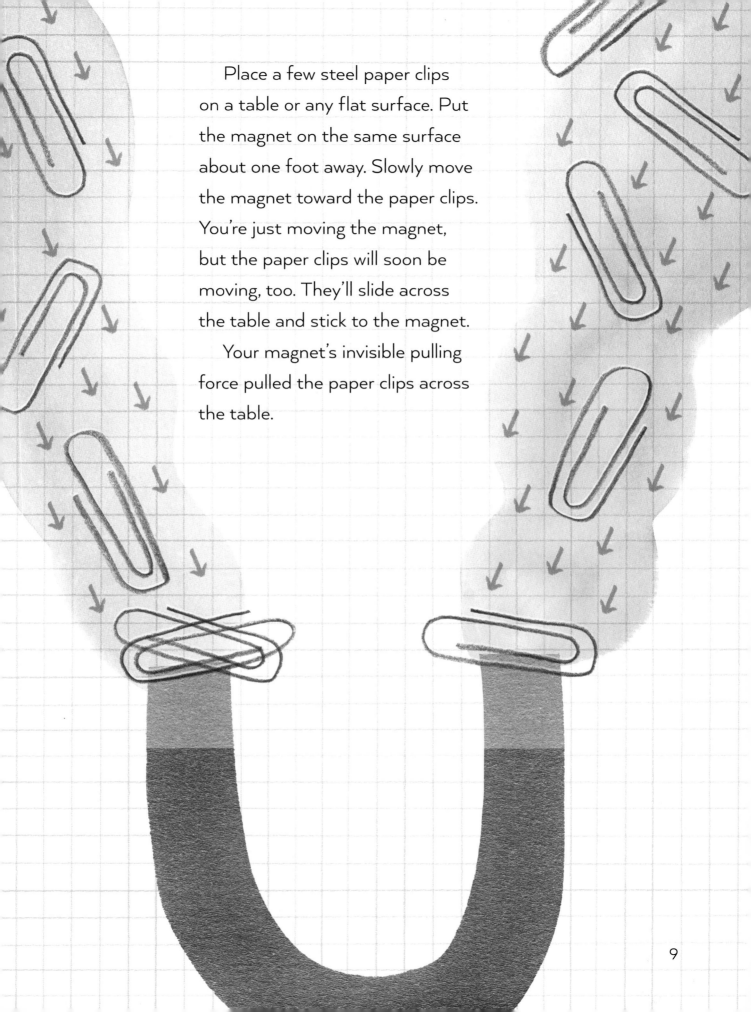

Place a few steel paper clips on a table or any flat surface. Put the magnet on the same surface about one foot away. Slowly move the magnet toward the paper clips. You're just moving the magnet, but the paper clips will soon be moving, too. They'll slide across the table and stick to the magnet.

Your magnet's invisible pulling force pulled the paper clips across the table.

9

If your magnet is strong enough, it will work through paper, water and glass.

Place a paper clip on a sheet of paper. Hold the magnet beneath the paper. Without ever touching the paper clip, you should be able to use your magnet to move it.

Drop a few paper clips in a shallow bowl of water. Hold your magnet at the surface of the water. If the magnet is strong enough it will pull the clips through the water.

With a really strong magnet you would be able to hold it against the side of the bowl and move the clips on the other side of the glass.

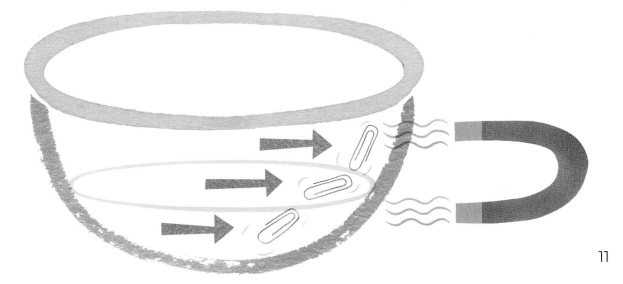

A bar magnet and some iron filings (available at most hardware stores) will help you understand magnetism.

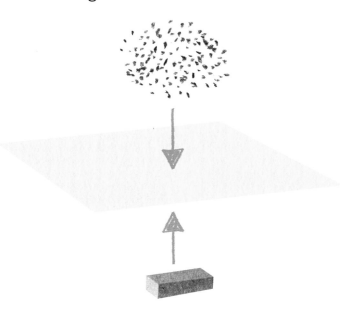

Cover your bar magnet with a white, unlined sheet of paper. Center the paper over the magnet. Sprinkle the iron filings onto the paper. Gently tap the paper.

Now look at the iron filings. They should form a pattern showing the magnet's *"magnetic field."* The pattern shows where the magnetic force is strongest. It's strongest by its two ends, where many of the filings should have gathered.

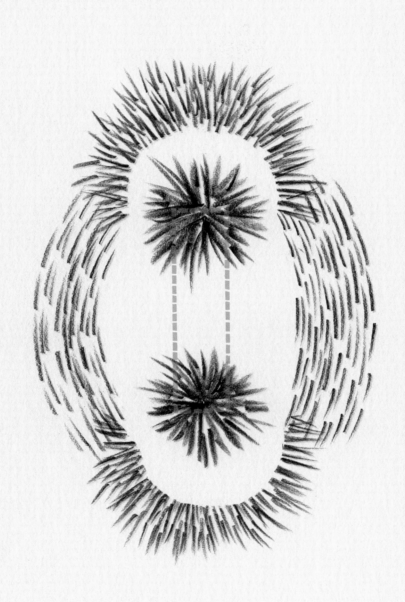

The two ends of a magnet are called its *"poles."* Each magnet has two poles, a north pole and a south pole.

You can test your bar magnet to see which is its north pole and which is its south pole.

Tie a thin string around the middle of the magnet going lengthwise. Tape the other end of the string to the bottom of a wooden bookshelf or table. The string should be just long enough to let the magnet hang freely. Be sure there are no other magnets nearby, nothing made of iron, steel, nickel or cobalt—nothing to confuse the magnet.

Gently tap the magnet. When it stops moving, one pole should be pointing north and the other pointing south.

Ask an adult which direction is north. With a marker, write "N" on that end of the magnet. Write "S" on the other end.

Sailors, hikers, pilots and others use compasses to help them find their way. The needle inside a compass is really a magnet. One end of the needle always points north.

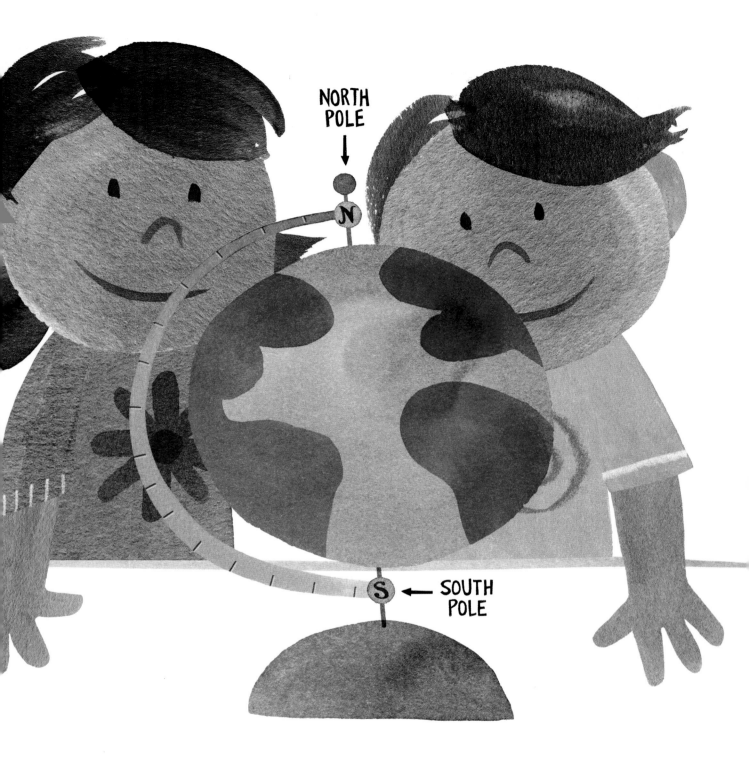

Look at any globe. The most northern part of the globe is labeled North Pole. The most southern part is labeled South Pole. The poles of every magnet always point north and south because the Earth is a huge magnet with a relatively weak magnetic field. Its magnetic pull is strongest at its two ends, its north and south poles.

With two bar magnets you can see how north and south poles *attract* and *repel* each other.

The poles of bar magnets are often marked N and S. If yours are not, you can test them by letting them hang freely, tapping them and then seeing which way each pole points. Then mark both ends of each magnet with an "N" and an "S."

Place both magnets on a table or any flat surface. Place them at least a foot apart. Line them up with one pole of each magnet facing the other. Slowly move each magnet toward the other.

If you have an "N" pole moving toward an "S" pole you'll feel a strong magnetic attraction between the magnets. The pole of one will stick to the pole of the other.

Opposite poles attract each other.

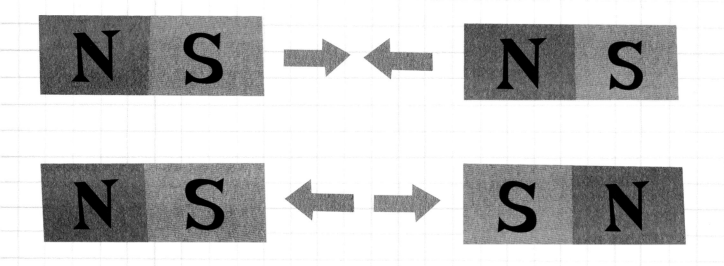

The only natural magnet is lodestone, a stone loaded with magnetite, a magnetic mineral. All other magnets are man-made.

You can make a magnet.

Take a large steel paper clip and hold it close to some iron filings. If the filings don't stick to the clip you know that the clip is not magnetic.

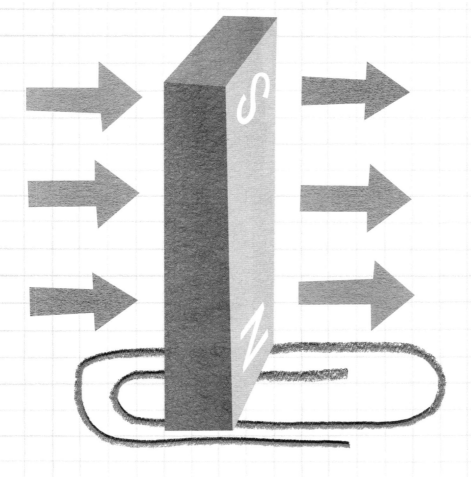

Now, take your bar magnet. Start with one pole of the magnet pressed against one end of the paper clip. Rub it along the clip to the other end. Do this again and again, twenty-five to thirty times. Rub the same pole of the magnet against the clip, always in the same direction.

Hold the large paper clip close to some iron filings. Does the clip attract the filings? If it does, the paper clip is now a magnet.

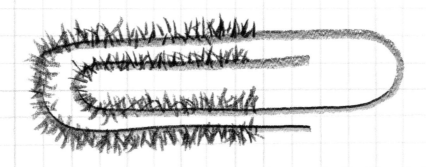

Why were you able to turn your paper clip into a magnet?

All metals are made of molecules, minuscule particles too small to see. Scientists tell us that the molecules that make up iron, steel, nickel and cobalt are tiny magnets that are normally a jumble.

When you rubbed the paper clip you aligned the tiny magnets until all the northern poles were pointing north, and all the southern poles were pointing south. With all the magnets lined up, the paper clip became one large magnet.

BEFORE

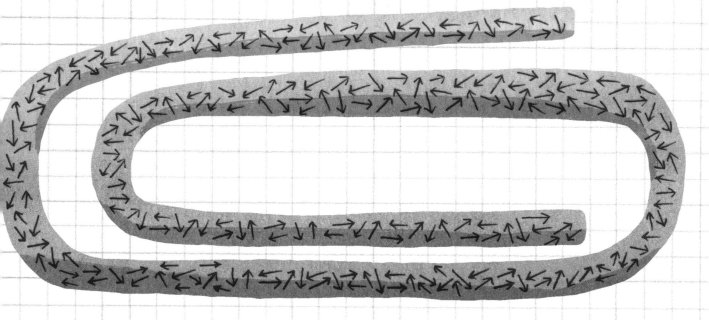

AFTER

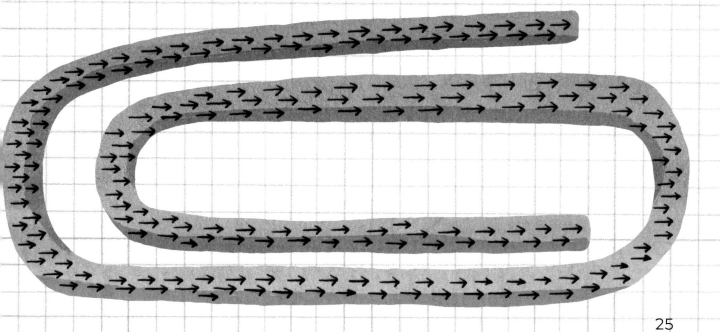

POW!

Magnets can lose their magnetic power when they are hit really hard or exposed to extreme heat.

26

Magnets can also multiply. When you break a magnet in half you create two smaller magnets, each with a north and south pole.

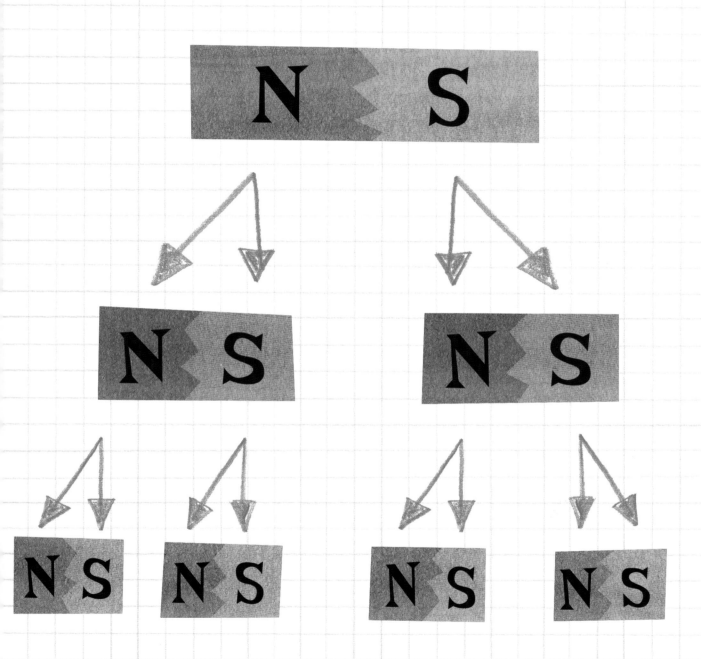

Electromagnets, sometimes called "on and off magnets," use electricity to create their magnetic fields.

When an electric current passes through a wire it creates only a weak magnetic field. Wrapping a wire with an electric current flowing through it around an iron rod turns the rod into a magnet. The tighter the coils of the wire—the more turns—and the stronger the electric current, the stronger the magnet.

If the electric current is turned off the electromagnet loses its power. That's why they're sometimes called "on and off magnets."

Electromagnets are used in buzzers and bells, computers, televisions and many other electric devices. They power all electric motors.

You can't see magnetism, but you can see what it does. It's difficult to imagine a world without magnets.

GLOSSARY

Attract – to pull toward

Electromagnet – a device that uses the flow of electricity to create a magnetic field

Force – the power to push or pull something

Magnetic field – the area around a magnet that attracts certain metals

Magnetism – the unseen power to pull and push certain metals

Pole – the point on a magnet where its magnetic force is strongest

Repel – to push away

Simple magnet – magnets that do not need an electric current to attract certain metals

INDEX

Aluminum, 7
Cell phone, 3
Cobalt, 4, 6, 15, 24
Coins, 6
Compass, 16
Computer, 3, 5, 31
Copper, 6
Electricity, 28, 29
Electromagnet, 5, 28, 29, 31, 32
Force, 8, 9, 32
　　　magnetic, 13
Glass, 10, 11
Heat, 26
Iron, 4, 6, 15, 24
　　　filings, 12, 13, 22, 23
Lodestone, 21
Magnetic field, 13, 17, 28, 29, 32
Microwave oven, 3

Molecule, 24
Nickel, 4, 6, 15, 24
North (direction), 15, 16, 25
Paper, 10, 12
Paperclip, 8, 9, 10, 11, 22, 23, 24, 25
Poles, 14, 15, 17, 19, 20, 21, 23, 25, 27, 32
　　　North, 14, 17, 18, 25, 27
　　　opposite, 21
　　　South, 15, 17, 18, 25, 27
Printer, 3
Simple magnet, 5
South (direction), 15, 25
Steel, 4, 6, 7, 9, 15, 22, 24
Television, 3, 5, 31
Vacuum cleaner, 3
Watch, 5
Water, 10, 11
Wire, 29